First
Facts®

Birds

Parrots

by Fran Howard

Consultant:
Tanya Dewey, PhD
University of Michigan Museum of Zoology
Ann Arbor, Michigan

CAPSTONE PRESS
a capstone imprint

First Facts is published by Capstone Press,
1710 Roe Crest Drive, North Mankato, Minnesota 56003.
www.capstonepub.com

Library of Congress Cataloging-in-Publication Data
Howard, Fran, 1953–
Parrots / by Fran Howard.
p. cm.—(First facts. birds.)
Includes bibliographical references and index.
Summary: "Discusses parrots, including their physical features, habitat, range,
and life cycle"—Provided by publisher.
ISBN 978-1-4296-8685-3 (library binding)
ISBN 978-1-62065-253-4 (ebook PDF)
1. Parrots—Juvenile literature. I. Title.
QL696.P7H689 2013
636.6'865—dc23   2012008041

Editorial Credits:

Lori Shores, editor; Juliette Peters, designer; Kathy McColley, production specialist

Photo Credits:

Alamy: Andrew Walmsley, 14, Juniors Bildarchiv, 19; Corbis: All Canada Photos/
Wayne Lynch, 6, Frank Lane Picture Agency/Hugh Clark/©FLPA, 13, Jim Zuckerman,
9; Dreamstime: Adam Goss, 10, David Davis, 5, Harmkruyshaar, 17, Katrina Brown, 21,
Latif1966, 1, Martingraf, 11; iStockphotos: cati laporte, 20; Shutterstock: UgputuLfSS,
cover

Artistic Effects

Shutterstock: ethylalkohol, Pavel K, pinare

Essential content terms are **bold** and are defined at the bottom of the page where they
first appear.

Printed in the United States of America in North Mankato, Minnesota.

042012   006682CGF12

Table of Contents

Colorful Birds

When it comes to colorful birds, parrots are superstars. These brightly colored birds really get noticed. Many parrots are green, but they can be almost any color.

The smallest parrots weigh just 2.25 ounces (64 grams). Large parrots weigh 3.5 pounds (1.6 kilograms). Parrots can be between 3.5 and 40 inches (8.9 and 102 centimeters) tall.

Parrot Fact!

Parrots and other birds have some hollow bones. Hollow bones make birds light and allow them to fly.

eyes

beak

wing

yellow-lored amazon

toes

5

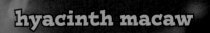
hyacinth macaw

Parrot Toes

Parrot feet are for more than walking. Parrots have two toes pointing forward and two pointing backward. Their toes help parrots **perch** on trees and rocks. Parrots also use their toes to hold food.

Parrot Fact!

Parrots are one of the few birds that eat with their feet.

perch—to sit on a high place to rest and view surroundings

Where Parrots Live

More than 350 kinds of parrots live around the world. Parrots are mostly found in **tropical** areas. Some parrots live in deserts and other hot, dry areas.

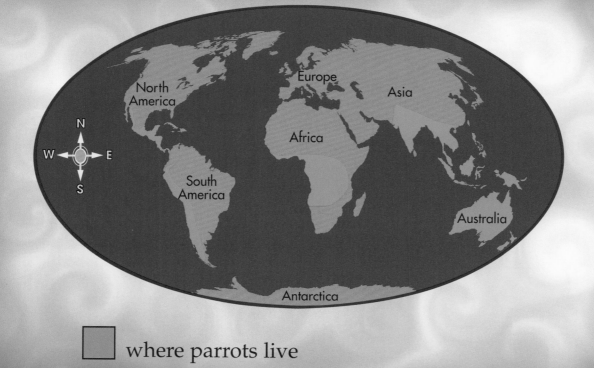

☐ where parrots live

scarlet macaw

Most parrots live in **rain forests**. Rain forests provide parrots with food and shelter. Parrots' colorful feathers help them blend in with flowers and fruit trees.

tropical—having to do with the hot and wet areas near the equator

rain forest—a thick forest where a great deal of rain falls

Hungry Parrots

Parrots are not picky eaters. They are **omnivores**, which means they eat both meat and plants. Parrots eat mostly seeds, nuts, and fruit. But they also catch and eat insects.

rainbow lorikeet

Australian king parrot (male)

Parrots use their hook-shaped beaks to grab food. They also use their strong beaks to crack open nuts.

Parrot Fact!

Lorikeets have little brushlike tongues. This type of tongue helps them eat nectar from flowers.

omnivore—an animal that eats plants and other animals

Parrot Nests

Before **mating**, parrots find places to nest. Most parrots make nests in hollow spaces in trees. They use natural holes or holes made by other animals. Some parrots use **burrows** left by other animals.

Parrot Fact!

Very few parrots make stick nests like many other birds.

mate—to join together to produce young

burrow—a tunnel or hole in the ground made or used by an animal

rose-ringed
parakeet

kea chicks

Parrot Families

Female parrots lay two to eight white eggs in their nests. Usually the female keeps the eggs warm. But some parrot parents take turns caring for eggs. In 17 to 35 days, the young parrots **hatch**.

hatch—to break out of an egg

Parrot Chicks

Newly hatched parrots are called chicks. They are covered in soft white **down**. Chicks cannot fly or find food until they grow adult feathers.

Both the male and female parrots care for their young. Chicks depend on their parents for food. Adult parrots chew up food before placing it in their chicks' mouths.

down—soft, fluffy feathers of a bird

Life Cycle of a Parrot

Newborn: Chicks hatch from eggs using a part of their beak called an egg tooth. This tooth later falls off.

Young: Young parrots stay in the nest between three weeks and four months.

young

Adult: Small parrots live between 15 and 20 years. Large parrots can live up to 80 years.

Danger!

Adult parrots have few **predators**. But snakes, wild cats, and monkeys eat parrot chicks. Some people catch wild parrots to sell as pets. In many countries it is against the law to catch wild parrots.

Parrot Fact!

Selling wild parrots is illegal in the United States.

predator—an animal that hunts other animals for food

blue and gold macaw

Parrots and People

Many people are fond of parrots. Wild parrots are protected in some national parks. Some people have pet parrots that were raised to be pets, not taken from the wild. Pet parrots need a lot of care and attention. They're not the right pet for everyone. But parrot owners say they're great companions.

African grey parrot

Amazing but True!

Moluccan cockatoo

Parrots are noisy! They squawk, shriek, and hoot. Parrots make sounds to warn each other of danger. They also make sounds to tell other parrots who they are. Pet parrots will copy sounds. They can learn to whistle or say words. Some parrots imitate ringing doorbells and phones!

21

Glossary

burrow (BUHR-oh)—a tunnel or hole in the ground made or used by an animal

down (DOUN)—soft, fluffy feathers of a bird

hatch (HACH)—to break out of an egg

mate (MATE)—to join together to produce young

omnivore (OM-nuh-vor)—an animal that eats plants and other animals

perch (PURCH)—to sit on a high place to rest and view surroundings

predator (PRED-uh-tur)—an animal that hunts other animals for food

rain forest (RAYN FOR-ist)—a thick forest where a great deal of rain falls

tropical (TRAH-pi-kuhl)—having to do with the hot and wet areas near the equator

Read More

Ganeri, Anita. *Macaw.* A Day in the Life: Rain Forest Animals. Chicago: Heinemann Library, 2011.

Owen, Ruth. *Parrots.* The World's Smartest Animals. New York: Windmill Books, 2012.

Rockwood, Leigh. *Parrots Are Smart!* Super Smart Animals. New York: PowerKids Press, 2010.

Internet Sites

FactHound offers a safe, fun way to find Internet sites related to this book. All of the sites on FactHound have been researched by our staff.

Here's all you do:

Visit *www.facthound.com*

Type in this code: 9781429686853

Index